# Pre-College
# BRAG BOOK

A guided space for 7th-12th graders
**TO CAPTURE KEY MOMENTS**
that supercharge future college essays

EASY early college prep!

by
J. Steele
Growth Story Press
Silicon Valley

## *Hello from Silicon Valley, I'm Julie!*

University of California scholarship **ESSAY INSIDER**

- I'm a graduate of UC Berkeley + application reader for incoming CAL students.
- Every year, I evaluate essays to help the university award scholarships to new freshman & transfer students.

Stanford **PARENT**

- I'm also the parent of a current Stanford undergraduate & graduate student.
- Using this growth story guidance, our daughter had great success with college applications and won multiple scholarships to help pay tuition.

## Brag Books were our GAME CHANGER!

Need a roadmap for successful college applications + scholarship awards?

 **8 INSIDER TIPS to know Early** (see page 106)

# 7th-12th graders!

EVERY college-prep student needs this **problem solver!**

## 1. WHAT is a Brag Book?

**A guided space** to collect special moments of growth & progress over the years.

I will guide you step-by-step to gather the growth stories, data points, personal wins, experiences & insights that evaluators look for in college essays.

## 2. WHY do I need a Brag Book?

When college applications approach, you'll be asked to write essays that rely on sharing your unique story – this Brag Book creates the personal story library you'll need (and wish you had).

Collecting your growth stories over time will build a valuable treasure chest of historical data and insights that can supercharge your future college essays.

With this essay treasure chest of story gold – Brag Books will boost confidence!

## 3. Why start NOW?

Time truly flies – will you remember *all* of your past noteworthy moments?

College essay prep (and worry) quickly ramps up **by 11th grade.**
**Hello 7th-10th graders** – this is only a few short years away.

College admissions are now more challenging (and stressful) than ever.

Creating your own personal story library early (meaning NOW) can significantly reduce the stress of college applications – and fuel more successful outcomes.

# CONTENTS

**AFTER completing each story** – **CREATE YOUR OWN "STORY INDEX" here** (to easily find extra special highlights later)

MY KEY HIGHLIGHTS:                                             page:

| | |
|---|---|
| | |
| | |
| | |
| | |
| | |
| | |

(tip: **sticky notes** make fast bookmarks)

| | |
|---|---|
| | |
| | |
| | |
| | |
| | |
| | |
| | |
| | |
| | |
| | |
| | |
| | |
| | |
| | |
| | |
| | |
| | |

(if you need more space ~ see last page of book)

# How to use this book in 3 easy steps

## 1. **Fill in the blanks** to turn a noteworthy personal experience into a GROWTH STORY to remember

- Helpful tips and questions will guide you!
- You don't have to fill in every box – only areas relevant to your story.
- See next page for examples of Growth Story moments, big and small.

## 2. **Insert documents you'd like to save** in between story pages to create a convenient FOLDER

- Photos, awards, congratulatory letters, event flyers, thank you notes, etc...
- You're collecting gold nuggets to fill a valuable treasure chest over time.

## 3. **Completed Brag Book = a *story library!***

- Building a story library gets you essay-ready, boosts confidence and lowers stress when college applications become the focus of 11th grade.
- This book includes guided pages for up to 49 stories.
- If you run out of pages, continue into another Brag Book to easily keep everything together.

TIPS > create your own Story Index (p.4) + sticky notes make fast bookmarks

# What is a GROWTH STORY?

**Any experience/event that marks a point of personal growth or insight.**

Examples of possible Growth Stories:

* a special problem you solved
* volunteer experience that inspired you to do more
* rewarding academic experience
* event you helped plan, host or organize – club, fundraiser, awareness etc.
* leadership experience or role (in or out of school)
* a personal win (or loss) leading to growth & deeper insights
* any award, special honor or recognition
* a new talent – or ongoing skill development
* passion project
* meaningful moments – including personal setbacks, struggles, obstacles
* special achievement or distinction
* mentoring, coaching or training someone
* community activity with special impact
* favorite hobby
* special performance
* part-time job
* career experience
* an important role or responsibility within your family (translator, childcare etc)
* a major lesson learned – or challenge faced
* **ANY** event that highlights your resilience, progress and/or determination

**NOTE:** Although only High School activities are included on college applications, essays can be enriched by longterm personal growth, interests and commitment that may have originated or sparked much earlier – **therefore Middle/JuniorHigh School is not too early to start tracking growth stories.**

# Don't forget about SUMMERS!

College applications, essay questions and campus interviewers often ask WHAT you did during the past 2 summers – and WHY.

Why are summers so important to colleges??? Summers help paint a picture of what matters to you – including what you choose to do when you have some free time.

NOTE: Summer activities are usually considered part of the next "rising" grade year
(so the summer between 9th & 10th grades is considered to be part of 10th grade).

# GROWTH STORY # 1

Answer any questions **relevant** to this story – **you do not have to fill in every box.**

**SHORT** title or keywords:

(for easy reference later when looking back on your special moments)

**DATES** to remember?

☐ School **YEAR**

☐ School **BREAK**

**ANY ORGANIZATIONS** involved?

(tracking orgs/groups can add important details to college applications + possibly lead to future scholarship opportunities related to certain groups)

**YOUR POSITION** or leadership role?

(past roles can reveal growth over time...like event planner, class rep, club leader, part-time job title, sports position, project leader, mentor etc)

**HOURS** spent per **WEEK**:

(this is required on most college applications so start tracking early... hours do NOT have to be exact, can be an average)

**KEY NUMBERS** to remember?

(data points add great context to a story...like how many people you helped, how many club members you led, how many event attendees, total $ funds raised, etc)

Special **ADVOCATES** to remember?

(your past supporters can someday turn into valuable Letters of Recommendation... for college, awards, and scholarships!)

## Keepsakes Folder!

**INSERT** any special documents between these two Story pages to create a convenient folder (photos, awards, thank you notes, event flyers, email printouts etc...also sticky notes with more details!)

# STORY NOTES - What happened?

Were you creative in some way?  Did you solve a problem?  Did you impact others in a positive way?
Did you practice leadership?  How did you grow or learn from this?  Anything else to remember?
(your personal insights + noteworthy data points can lead to amazing future college essays)

# GROWTH STORY # 2

Answer any questions **relevant** to this story – **you do not have to fill in every box.**

**SHORT**
title or
keywords:

(for easy reference later
when looking back on
your special moments)

**DATES**
to remember?

☐ School **YEAR**

☐ School **BREAK**

**ANY
ORGANIZATIONS**
involved?

(tracking orgs/groups
can add important details
to college applications
+ possibly lead to future
scholarship opportunities
related to certain groups)

**YOUR
POSITION**
or leadership
role?

(past roles can reveal
growth over time...like
event planner, class rep,
club leader, part-time
job title, sports position,
project leader, mentor etc)

**HOURS** spent
per **WEEK:**

(this is required on most
college applications
so start tracking early...
hours do NOT have to be
exact, can be an average)

**KEY
NUMBERS**
to remember?

(data points add great
context to a story...like
how many people you
helped, how many club
members you led, how
many event attendees,
total $ funds raised, etc)

Special
**ADVOCATES**
to remember?

(your past supporters
can someday turn into
valuable Letters of
Recommendation...
for college, awards,
and scholarships!)

**Keepsakes
Folder!**

10

**INSERT** any special documents between these two Story pages
to create a convenient folder (photos, awards, thank you notes,
event flyers, email printouts etc...also sticky notes with more details!)

# STORY NOTES - What happened?

Were you creative in some way?  Did you solve a problem?  Did you impact others in a positive way?
Did you practice leadership?  How did you grow or learn from this?  Anything else to remember?
(your personal insights + noteworthy data points can lead to amazing future college essays)

# GROWTH STORY  # 3

Answer any questions **relevant** to this story – **you do not have to fill in every box.**

**SHORT** title or keywords:

(for easy reference later when looking back on your special moments)

**DATES** to remember?

☐ School **YEAR**

☐ School **BREAK**

**ANY ORGANIZATIONS** involved?

(tracking orgs/groups can add important details to college applications + possibly lead to future scholarship opportunities related to certain groups)

**YOUR POSITION** or leadership role?

(past roles can reveal growth over time...like event planner, class rep, club leader, part-time job title, sports position, project leader, mentor etc)

**HOURS spent** per **WEEK:**

(this is required on most college applications so start tracking early... hours do NOT have to be exact, can be an average)

**KEY NUMBERS** to remember?

(data points add great context to a story...like how many people you helped, how many club members you led, how many event attendees, total $ funds raised, etc)

Special **ADVOCATES** to remember?

(your past supporters can someday turn into valuable Letters of Recommendation... for college, awards, and scholarships!)

**Keepsakes Folder!**

**INSERT** any special documents between these two Story pages to create a convenient folder (photos, awards, thank you notes, event flyers, email printouts etc...also sticky notes with more details!)

# STORY NOTES - What happened?

Were you creative in some way?  Did you solve a problem?  Did you impact others in a positive way?
Did you practice leadership?  How did you grow or learn from this?  Anything else to remember?
(your personal insights + noteworthy data points can lead to amazing future college essays)

# GROWTH STORY # 4

Answer any questions **relevant** to this story – **you do not have to fill in every box.**

**SHORT** title or keywords:

(for easy reference later when looking back on your special moments)

**DATES** to remember?

☐ School **YEAR**

☐ School **BREAK**

**ANY ORGANIZATIONS** involved?

(tracking orgs/groups can add important details to college applications + possibly lead to future scholarship opportunities related to certain groups)

**YOUR POSITION** or leadership role?

(past roles can reveal growth over time...like event planner, class rep, club leader, part-time job title, sports position, project leader, mentor etc)

**HOURS spent per WEEK:**

(this is required on most college applications so start tracking early... hours do NOT have to be exact, can be an average)

**KEY NUMBERS** to remember?

(data points add great context to a story...like how many people you helped, how many club members you led, how many event attendees, total $ funds raised, etc)

Special **ADVOCATES** to remember?

(your past supporters can someday turn into valuable Letters of Recommendation... for college, awards, and scholarships!)

 **Keepsakes Folder!**

14

**INSERT** any special documents between these two Story pages to create a convenient folder (photos, awards, thank you notes, event flyers, email printouts etc...also sticky notes with more details!)

## STORY NOTES - What happened?

Were you creative in some way?  Did you solve a problem?  Did you impact others in a positive way?
Did you practice leadership?  How did you grow or learn from this?  Anything else to remember?
(your personal insights + noteworthy data points can lead to amazing future college essays)

# GROWTH STORY # 5

Answer any questions **relevant** to this story – **you do not have to fill in every box.**

**SHORT** title or keywords:

(for easy reference later when looking back on your special moments)

**DATES** to remember?

☐ School **YEAR**

☐ School **BREAK**

**ANY ORGANIZATIONS** involved?

(tracking orgs/groups can add important details to college applications + possibly lead to future scholarship opportunities related to certain groups)

**YOUR POSITION** or leadership role?

(past roles can reveal growth over time...like event planner, class rep, club leader, part-time job title, sports position, project leader, mentor etc)

**HOURS spent** per **WEEK:**

(this is required on most college applications so start tracking early... hours do NOT have to be exact, can be an average)

**KEY NUMBERS** to remember?

(data points add great context to a story...like how many people you helped, how many club members you led, how many event attendees, total $ funds raised, etc)

Special **ADVOCATES** to remember?

(your past supporters can someday turn into valuable Letters of Recommendation... for college, awards, and scholarships!)

**Keepsakes Folder!**

**INSERT** any special documents between these two Story pages to create a convenient folder (photos, awards, thank you notes, event flyers, email printouts etc...also sticky notes with more details!)

## STORY NOTES - What happened?

Were you creative in some way?  Did you solve a problem?  Did you impact others in a positive way?
Did you practice leadership?  How did you grow or learn from this?  Anything else to remember?
(your personal insights + noteworthy data points can lead to amazing future college essays)

# GROWTH STORY # 6

Answer any questions **relevant** to this story – **you do not have to fill in every box.**

**SHORT title or keywords:**

(for easy reference later when looking back on your special moments)

**DATES to remember?**

☐ School **YEAR**

☐ School **BREAK**

**ANY ORGANIZATIONS involved?**

(tracking orgs/groups can add important details to college applications + possibly lead to future scholarship opportunities related to certain groups)

**YOUR POSITION or leadership role?**

(past roles can reveal growth over time...like event planner, class rep, club leader, part-time job title, sports position, project leader, mentor etc)

**HOURS spent per WEEK:**

(this is required on most college applications so start tracking early... hours do NOT have to be exact, can be an average)

**KEY NUMBERS to remember?**

(data points add great context to a story...like how many people you helped, how many club members you led, how many event attendees, total $ funds raised, etc)

**Special ADVOCATES to remember?**

(your past supporters can someday turn into valuable Letters of Recommendation... for college, awards, and scholarships!)

**Keepsakes Folder!**

18

**INSERT** any special documents between these two Story pages to create a convenient folder (photos, awards, thank you notes, event flyers, email printouts etc...also sticky notes with more details!)

# STORY NOTES - What happened?

Were you creative in some way?  Did you solve a problem?  Did you impact others in a positive way?
Did you practice leadership?  How did you grow or learn from this?  Anything else to remember?
(your personal insights + noteworthy data points can lead to amazing future college essays)

# GROWTH STORY # 7

Answer any questions **relevant** to this story – **you do not have to fill in every box.**

**SHORT** title or keywords:

(for easy reference later when looking back on your special moments)

**DATES** to remember?

☐ School **YEAR**

☐ School **BREAK**

**ANY ORGANIZATIONS** involved?

(tracking orgs/groups can add important details to college applications + possibly lead to future scholarship opportunities related to certain groups)

**YOUR POSITION** or leadership role?

(past roles can reveal growth over time...like event planner, class rep, club leader, part-time job title, sports position, project leader, mentor etc)

**HOURS spent** per **WEEK:**

(this is required on most college applications so start tracking early... hours do NOT have to be exact, can be an average)

**KEY NUMBERS** to remember?

(data points add great context to a story...like how many people you helped, how many club members you led, how many event attendees, total $ funds raised, etc)

Special **ADVOCATES** to remember?

(your past supporters can someday turn into valuable Letters of Recommendation... for college, awards, and scholarships!)

**Keepsakes Folder!**

20

**INSERT** any special documents between these two Story pages to create a convenient folder (photos, awards, thank you notes, event flyers, email printouts etc...also sticky notes with more details!)

# STORY NOTES - What happened?

Were you creative in some way?  Did you solve a problem?  Did you impact others in a positive way?
Did you practice leadership?  How did you grow or learn from this?  Anything else to remember?
(your personal insights + noteworthy data points can lead to amazing future college essays)

# GROWTH STORY # 8

Answer any questions **relevant** to this story – **you do not have to fill in every box.**

**SHORT title or keywords:**

(for easy reference later when looking back on your special moments)

**DATES to remember?**

☐ School **YEAR**

☐ School **BREAK**

**ANY ORGANIZATIONS involved?**

(tracking orgs/groups can add important details to college applications + possibly lead to future scholarship opportunities related to certain groups)

**YOUR POSITION or leadership role?**

(past roles can reveal growth over time...like event planner, class rep, club leader, part-time job title, sports position, project leader, mentor etc)

**HOURS spent per WEEK:**

(this is required on most college applications so start tracking early... hours do NOT have to be exact, can be an average)

**KEY NUMBERS to remember?**

(data points add great context to a story...like how many people you helped, how many club members you led, how many event attendees, total $ funds raised, etc)

**Special ADVOCATES to remember?**

(your past supporters can someday turn into valuable Letters of Recommendation... for college, awards, and scholarships!)

# Keepsakes Folder!

22

**INSERT** any special documents between these two Story pages to create a convenient folder (photos, awards, thank you notes, event flyers, email printouts etc...also sticky notes with more details!)

## STORY NOTES - What happened?

Were you creative in some way?  Did you solve a problem?  Did you impact others in a positive way?
Did you practice leadership?  How did you grow or learn from this?  Anything else to remember?
(your personal insights + noteworthy data points can lead to amazing future college essays)

# GROWTH STORY # 9

Answer any questions **relevant** to this story – **you do not have to fill in every box.**

**SHORT title or keywords:**

(for easy reference later when looking back on your special moments)

**DATES to remember?**

☐ School **YEAR**

☐ School **BREAK**

**ANY ORGANIZATIONS involved?**

(tracking orgs/groups can add important details to college applications + possibly lead to future scholarship opportunities related to certain groups)

**YOUR POSITION or leadership role?**

(past roles can reveal growth over time...like event planner, class rep, club leader, part-time job title, sports position, project leader, mentor etc)

**HOURS spent per WEEK:**

(this is required on most college applications so start tracking early... hours do NOT have to be exact, can be an average)

**KEY NUMBERS to remember?**

(data points add great context to a story...like how many people you helped, how many club members you led, how many event attendees, total $ funds raised, etc)

**Special ADVOCATES to remember?**

(your past supporters can someday turn into valuable Letters of Recommendation... for college, awards, and scholarships!)

**Keepsakes Folder!**

**INSERT** any special documents between these two Story pages to create a convenient folder (photos, awards, thank you notes, event flyers, email printouts etc...also sticky notes with more details!)

# STORY NOTES - What happened?

Were you creative in some way?  Did you solve a problem?  Did you impact others in a positive way?
Did you practice leadership?  How did you grow or learn from this?  Anything else to remember?
(your personal insights + noteworthy data points can lead to amazing future college essays)

# GROWTH STORY # 10

Answer any questions **relevant** to this story – **you do not have to fill in every box.**

**SHORT** title or keywords:

(for easy reference later when looking back on your special moments)

**DATES** to remember?

☐ School **YEAR**

☐ School **BREAK**

**ANY ORGANIZATIONS** involved?

(tracking orgs/groups can add important details to college applications + possibly lead to future scholarship opportunities related to certain groups)

**YOUR POSITION** or leadership role?

(past roles can reveal growth over time...like event planner, class rep, club leader, part-time job title, sports position, project leader, mentor etc)

**HOURS** spent per **WEEK:**

(this is required on most college applications so start tracking early... hours do NOT have to be exact, can be an average)

**KEY NUMBERS** to remember?

(data points add great context to a story...like how many people you helped, how many club members you led, how many event attendees, total $ funds raised, etc)

Special **ADVOCATES** to remember?

(your past supporters can someday turn into valuable Letters of Recommendation... for college, awards, and scholarships!)

**Keepsakes Folder!**

26

**INSERT** any special documents between these two Story pages to create a convenient folder (photos, awards, thank you notes, event flyers, email printouts etc...also sticky notes with more details!)

# STORY NOTES - What happened?

Were you creative in some way?  Did you solve a problem?  Did you impact others in a positive way? Did you practice leadership?  How did you grow or learn from this?  Anything else to remember? (your personal insights + noteworthy data points can lead to amazing future college essays)

# GROWTH STORY # 11

Answer any questions **relevant** to this story – **you do not have to fill in every box.**

**SHORT title or keywords:**

(for easy reference later when looking back on your special moments)

**DATES to remember?**

☐ School **YEAR**

☐ School **BREAK**

**ANY ORGANIZATIONS involved?**

(tracking orgs/groups can add important details to college applications + possibly lead to future scholarship opportunities related to certain groups)

**YOUR POSITION or leadership role?**

(past roles can reveal growth over time...like event planner, class rep, club leader, part-time job title, sports position, project leader, mentor etc)

**HOURS spent per WEEK:**

(this is required on most college applications so start tracking early... hours do NOT have to be exact, can be an average)

**KEY NUMBERS to remember?**

(data points add great context to a story...like how many people you helped, how many club members you led, how many event attendees, total $ funds raised, etc)

**Special ADVOCATES to remember?**

(your past supporters can someday turn into valuable Letters of Recommendation... for college, awards, and scholarships!)

**Keepsakes Folder!**

**28**

**INSERT** any special documents between these two Story pages to create a convenient folder (photos, awards, thank you notes, event flyers, email printouts etc...also sticky notes with more details!)

# STORY NOTES - What happened?

Were you creative in some way?  Did you solve a problem?  Did you impact others in a positive way?
Did you practice leadership?  How did you grow or learn from this?  Anything else to remember?
(your personal insights + noteworthy data points can lead to amazing future college essays)

# GROWTH STORY # 12

Answer any questions **relevant** to this story – **you do not have to fill in every box.**

**SHORT title or keywords:**

(for easy reference later when looking back on your special moments)

**DATES to remember?**

☐ School **YEAR**

☐ School **BREAK**

**ANY ORGANIZATIONS involved?**

(tracking orgs/groups can add important details to college applications + possibly lead to future scholarship opportunities related to certain groups)

**YOUR POSITION or leadership role?**

(past roles can reveal growth over time...like event planner, class rep, club leader, part-time job title, sports position, project leader, mentor etc)

**HOURS spent per WEEK:**

(this is required on most college applications so start tracking early... hours do NOT have to be exact, can be an average)

**KEY NUMBERS to remember?**

(data points add great context to a story...like how many people you helped, how many club members you led, how many event attendees, total $ funds raised, etc)

**Special ADVOCATES to remember?**

(your past supporters can someday turn into valuable Letters of Recommendation... for college, awards, and scholarships!)

**Keepsakes Folder!**

30

**INSERT** any special documents between these two Story pages to create a convenient folder (photos, awards, thank you notes, event flyers, email printouts etc...also sticky notes with more details!)

# STORY NOTES - What happened?

Were you creative in some way?  Did you solve a problem?  Did you impact others in a positive way?
Did you practice leadership?  How did you grow or learn from this?  Anything else to remember?
(your personal insights + noteworthy data points can lead to amazing future college essays)

# GROWTH STORY # 13

Answer any questions **relevant** to this story – **you do not have to fill in every box.**

**SHORT** title or keywords:

(for easy reference later when looking back on your special moments)

**DATES** to remember?

☐ School **YEAR**

☐ School **BREAK**

**ANY ORGANIZATIONS** involved?

(tracking orgs/groups can add important details to college applications + possibly lead to future scholarship opportunities related to certain groups)

**YOUR POSITION** or leadership role?

(past roles can reveal growth over time...like event planner, class rep, club leader, part-time job title, sports position, project leader, mentor etc)

**HOURS** spent per **WEEK:**

(this is required on most college applications so start tracking early... hours do NOT have to be exact, can be an average)

**KEY NUMBERS** to remember?

(data points add great context to a story...like how many people you helped, how many club members you led, how many event attendees, total $ funds raised, etc)

Special **ADVOCATES** to remember?

(your past supporters can someday turn into valuable Letters of Recommendation... for college, awards, and scholarships!)

**Keepsakes Folder!**

**INSERT** any special documents between these two Story pages to create a convenient folder (photos, awards, thank you notes, event flyers, email printouts etc...also sticky notes with more details!)

32

# STORY NOTES - What happened?

Were you creative in some way?  Did you solve a problem?  Did you impact others in a positive way?
Did you practice leadership?  How did you grow or learn from this?  Anything else to remember?
(your personal insights + noteworthy data points can lead to amazing future college essays)

# GROWTH STORY # 14

Answer any questions **relevant** to this story – **you do not have to fill in every box.**

**SHORT** title or keywords:

(for easy reference later when looking back on your special moments)

**DATES** to remember?

☐ School **YEAR**

☐ School **BREAK**

**ANY ORGANIZATIONS** involved?

(tracking orgs/groups can add important details to college applications + possibly lead to future scholarship opportunities related to certain groups)

**YOUR POSITION** or leadership role?

(past roles can reveal growth over time...like event planner, class rep, club leader, part-time job title, sports position, project leader, mentor etc)

**HOURS** spent per **WEEK:**

(this is required on most college applications so start tracking early... hours do NOT have to be exact, can be an average)

**KEY NUMBERS** to remember?

(data points add great context to a story...like how many people you helped, how many club members you led, how many event attendees, total $ funds raised, etc)

Special **ADVOCATES** to remember?

(your past supporters can someday turn into valuable Letters of Recommendation... for college, awards, and scholarships!)

**Keepsakes Folder!**

34

**INSERT** any special documents between these two Story pages to create a convenient folder (photos, awards, thank you notes, event flyers, email printouts etc...also sticky notes with more details!)

# STORY NOTES - What happened?

Were you creative in some way?  Did you solve a problem?  Did you impact others in a positive way?
Did you practice leadership?  How did you grow or learn from this?  Anything else to remember?
(your personal insights + noteworthy data points can lead to amazing future college essays)

# GROWTH STORY # 15

Answer any questions **relevant** to this story – **you do not have to fill in every box.**

**SHORT** title or keywords:

(for easy reference later when looking back on your special moments)

**DATES** to remember?

☐ School **YEAR**

☐ School **BREAK**

**ANY ORGANIZATIONS** involved?

(tracking orgs/groups can add important details to college applications + possibly lead to future scholarship opportunities related to certain groups)

**YOUR POSITION** or leadership role?

(past roles can reveal growth over time...like event planner, class rep, club leader, part-time job title, sports position, project leader, mentor etc)

**HOURS** spent per **WEEK:**

(this is required on most college applications so start tracking early... hours do NOT have to be exact, can be an average)

**KEY NUMBERS** to remember?

(data points add great context to a story...like how many people you helped, how many club members you led, how many event attendees, total $ funds raised, etc)

Special **ADVOCATES** to remember?

(your past supporters can someday turn into valuable Letters of Recommendation... for college, awards, and scholarships!)

## Keepsakes Folder!

**INSERT** any special documents between these two Story pages to create a convenient folder (photos, awards, thank you notes, event flyers, email printouts etc...also sticky notes with more details!)

# STORY NOTES - What happened?

Were you creative in some way?  Did you solve a problem?  Did you impact others in a positive way?
Did you practice leadership?  How did you grow or learn from this?  Anything else to remember?
(your personal insights + noteworthy data points can lead to amazing future college essays)

# GROWTH STORY # 16

Answer any questions **relevant** to this story – **you do not have to fill in every box.**

**SHORT title or keywords:**

(for easy reference later when looking back on your special moments)

**DATES to remember?**

☐ School **YEAR**

☐ School **BREAK**

**ANY ORGANIZATIONS involved?**

(tracking orgs/groups can add important details to college applications + possibly lead to future scholarship opportunities related to certain groups)

**YOUR POSITION or leadership role?**

(past roles can reveal growth over time...like event planner, class rep, club leader, part-time job title, sports position, project leader, mentor etc)

**HOURS spent per WEEK:**

(this is required on most college applications so start tracking early... hours do NOT have to be exact, can be an average)

**KEY NUMBERS to remember?**

(data points add great context to a story...like how many people you helped, how many club members you led, how many event attendees, total $ funds raised, etc)

**Special ADVOCATES to remember?**

(your past supporters can someday turn into valuable Letters of Recommendation... for college, awards, and scholarships!)

# Keepsakes
# Folder!

**38**

**INSERT** any special documents between these two Story pages to create a convenient folder (photos, awards, thank you notes, event flyers, email printouts etc...also sticky notes with more details!)

# STORY NOTES - What happened?

Were you creative in some way?  Did you solve a problem?  Did you impact others in a positive way?
Did you practice leadership?  How did you grow or learn from this?  Anything else to remember?
(your personal insights + noteworthy data points can lead to amazing future college essays)

# GROWTH STORY # 17

Answer any questions **relevant** to this story – **you do not have to fill in every box.**

**SHORT title or keywords:**

(for easy reference later when looking back on your special moments)

**DATES to remember?**

☐ School **YEAR**

☐ School **BREAK**

**ANY ORGANIZATIONS involved?**

(tracking orgs/groups can add important details to college applications + possibly lead to future scholarship opportunities related to certain groups)

**YOUR POSITION or leadership role?**

(past roles can reveal growth over time...like event planner, class rep, club leader, part-time job title, sports position, project leader, mentor etc)

**HOURS spent per WEEK:**

(this is required on most college applications so start tracking early... hours do NOT have to be exact, can be an average)

**KEY NUMBERS to remember?**

(data points add great context to a story...like how many people you helped, how many club members you led, how many event attendees, total $ funds raised, etc)

**Special ADVOCATES to remember?**

(your past supporters can someday turn into valuable Letters of Recommendation... for college, awards, and scholarships!)

**Keepsakes Folder!**

40

**INSERT** any special documents between these two Story pages to create a convenient folder (photos, awards, thank you notes, event flyers, email printouts etc...also sticky notes with more details!)

## STORY NOTES - What happened?

Were you creative in some way?  Did you solve a problem?  Did you impact others in a positive way?
Did you practice leadership?  How did you grow or learn from this?  Anything else to remember?
(your personal insights + noteworthy data points can lead to amazing future college essays)

# GROWTH STORY # 18

Answer any questions **relevant** to this story – **you do not have to fill in every box.**

**SHORT** title or keywords:

(for easy reference later when looking back on your special moments)

**DATES** to remember?

☐ School **YEAR**

☐ School **BREAK**

**ANY ORGANIZATIONS** involved?

(tracking orgs/groups can add important details to college applications + possibly lead to future scholarship opportunities related to certain groups)

**YOUR POSITION** or leadership role?

(past roles can reveal growth over time...like event planner, class rep, club leader, part-time job title, sports position, project leader, mentor etc)

**HOURS spent** per **WEEK:**

(this is required on most college applications so start tracking early... hours do NOT have to be exact, can be an average)

**KEY NUMBERS** to remember?

(data points add great context to a story...like how many people you helped, how many club members you led, how many event attendees, total $ funds raised, etc)

Special **ADVOCATES** to remember?

(your past supporters can someday turn into valuable Letters of Recommendation... for college, awards, and scholarships!)

**Keepsakes Folder!**

42

**INSERT** any special documents between these two Story pages to create a convenient folder (photos, awards, thank you notes, event flyers, email printouts etc...also sticky notes with more details!)

## STORY NOTES - What happened?

Were you creative in some way?  Did you solve a problem?  Did you impact others in a positive way?
Did you practice leadership?  How did you grow or learn from this?  Anything else to remember?
(your personal insights + noteworthy data points can lead to amazing future college essays)

# GROWTH STORY # 19

Answer any questions **relevant** to this story – **you do not have to fill in every box.**

**SHORT** title or keywords:

(for easy reference later when looking back on your special moments)

**DATES** to remember?

☐ School **YEAR**

☐ School **BREAK**

**ANY ORGANIZATIONS** involved?

(tracking orgs/groups can add important details to college applications + possibly lead to future scholarship opportunities related to certain groups)

**YOUR POSITION** or leadership role?

(past roles can reveal growth over time...like event planner, class rep, club leader, part-time job title, sports position, project leader, mentor etc)

**HOURS spent** per **WEEK:**

(this is required on most college applications so start tracking early... hours do NOT have to be exact, can be an average)

**KEY NUMBERS** to remember?

(data points add great context to a story...like how many people you helped, how many club members you led, how many event attendees, total $ funds raised, etc)

Special **ADVOCATES** to remember?

(your past supporters can someday turn into valuable Letters of Recommendation... for college, awards, and scholarships!)

**Keepsakes Folder!**

**INSERT** any special documents between these two Story pages to create a convenient folder (photos, awards, thank you notes, event flyers, email printouts etc...also sticky notes with more details!)

44

# STORY NOTES - What happened?

Were you creative in some way?  Did you solve a problem?  Did you impact others in a positive way?
Did you practice leadership?  How did you grow or learn from this?  Anything else to remember?
(your personal insights + noteworthy data points can lead to amazing future college essays)

# GROWTH STORY # 20

Answer any questions **relevant** to this story – **you do not have to fill in every box.**

**SHORT title or keywords:**

(for easy reference later when looking back on your special moments)

**DATES to remember?**

☐ School **YEAR**

☐ School **BREAK**

**ANY ORGANIZATIONS involved?**

(tracking orgs/groups can add important details to college applications + possibly lead to future scholarship opportunities related to certain groups)

**YOUR POSITION or leadership role?**

(past roles can reveal growth over time...like event planner, class rep, club leader, part-time job title, sports position, project leader, mentor etc)

**HOURS spent per WEEK:**

(this is required on most college applications so start tracking early... hours do NOT have to be exact, can be an average)

**KEY NUMBERS to remember?**

(data points add great context to a story...like how many people you helped, how many club members you led, how many event attendees, total $ funds raised, etc)

**Special ADVOCATES to remember?**

(your past supporters can someday turn into valuable Letters of Recommendation... for college, awards, and scholarships!)

**Keepsakes Folder!**

46

**INSERT** any special documents between these two Story pages to create a convenient folder (photos, awards, thank you notes, event flyers, email printouts etc...also sticky notes with more details!)

# STORY NOTES - What happened?

Were you creative in some way?  Did you solve a problem?  Did you impact others in a positive way?
Did you practice leadership?  How did you grow or learn from this?  Anything else to remember?
(your personal insights + noteworthy data points can lead to amazing future college essays)

# GROWTH STORY # 21

Answer any questions **relevant** to this story – **you do not have to fill in every box.**

**SHORT**
title or
keywords:

(for easy reference later
when looking back on
your special moments)

**DATES**
to remember?

☐ School **YEAR**

☐ School **BREAK**

**ANY**
**ORGANIZATIONS**
involved?

(tracking orgs/groups
can add important details
to college applications
+ possibly lead to future
scholarship opportunities
related to certain groups)

**YOUR**
**POSITION**
or leadership
role?

(past roles can reveal
growth over time...like
event planner, class rep,
club leader, part-time
job title, sports position,
project leader, mentor etc)

**HOURS** spent
per **WEEK:**

(this is required on most
college applications
so start tracking early...
hours do NOT have to be
exact, can be an average)

**KEY**
**NUMBERS**
to remember?

(data points add great
context to a story...like
how many people you
helped, how many club
members you led, how
many event attendees,
total $ funds raised, etc)

Special
**ADVOCATES**
to remember?

(your past supporters
can someday turn into
valuable Letters of
Recommendation...
for college, awards,
and scholarships!)

**Keepsakes Folder!**

**INSERT** any special documents between these two Story pages
to create a convenient folder (photos, awards, thank you notes,
event flyers, email printouts etc...also sticky notes with more details!)

## STORY NOTES - What happened?

Were you creative in some way?  Did you solve a problem?  Did you impact others in a positive way?
Did you practice leadership?  How did you grow or learn from this?  Anything else to remember?
(your personal insights + noteworthy data points can lead to amazing future college essays)

# GROWTH STORY # 22

Answer any questions **relevant** to this story – **you do not have to fill in every box.**

**SHORT** title or keywords:

(for easy reference later when looking back on your special moments)

**DATES** to remember?

☐ School **YEAR**

☐ School **BREAK**

**ANY ORGANIZATIONS** involved?

(tracking orgs/groups can add important details to college applications + possibly lead to future scholarship opportunities related to certain groups)

**YOUR POSITION** or leadership role?

(past roles can reveal growth over time...like event planner, class rep, club leader, part-time job title, sports position, project leader, mentor etc)

**HOURS** spent per **WEEK:**

(this is required on most college applications so start tracking early... hours do NOT have to be exact, can be an average)

**KEY NUMBERS** to remember?

(data points add great context to a story...like how many people you helped, how many club members you led, how many event attendees, total $ funds raised, etc)

Special **ADVOCATES** to remember?

(your past supporters can someday turn into valuable Letters of Recommendation... for college, awards, and scholarships!)

**Keepsakes Folder!**

50

**INSERT** any special documents between these two Story pages to create a convenient folder (photos, awards, thank you notes, event flyers, email printouts etc...also sticky notes with more details!)

# STORY NOTES - What happened?

Were you creative in some way?  Did you solve a problem?  Did you impact others in a positive way?
Did you practice leadership?  How did you grow or learn from this?  Anything else to remember?
(your personal insights + noteworthy data points can lead to amazing future college essays)

# GROWTH STORY # 23

Answer any questions **relevant** to this story – **you do not have to fill in every box.**

**SHORT** title or keywords:

(for easy reference later when looking back on your special moments)

**DATES** to remember?

☐ School **YEAR**

☐ School **BREAK**

**ANY ORGANIZATIONS** involved?

(tracking orgs/groups can add important details to college applications + possibly lead to future scholarship opportunities related to certain groups)

**YOUR POSITION** or leadership role?

(past roles can reveal growth over time...like event planner, class rep, club leader, part-time job title, sports position, project leader, mentor etc)

**HOURS** spent per **WEEK**:

(this is required on most college applications so start tracking early... hours do NOT have to be exact, can be an average)

**KEY NUMBERS** to remember?

(data points add great context to a story...like how many people you helped, how many club members you led, how many event attendees, total $ funds raised, etc)

Special **ADVOCATES** to remember?

(your past supporters can someday turn into valuable Letters of Recommendation... for college, awards, and scholarships!)

**Keepsakes Folder!**

52

**INSERT** any special documents between these two Story pages to create a convenient folder (photos, awards, thank you notes, event flyers, email printouts etc...also sticky notes with more details!)

# STORY NOTES - What happened?

Were you creative in some way?  Did you solve a problem?  Did you impact others in a positive way?
Did you practice leadership?  How did you grow or learn from this?  Anything else to remember?
(your personal insights + noteworthy data points can lead to amazing future college essays)

# GROWTH STORY # 24

Answer any questions **relevant** to this story – **you do not have to fill in every box.**

**SHORT title or keywords:**

(for easy reference later when looking back on your special moments)

**DATES to remember?**

☐ School **YEAR**

☐ School **BREAK**

**ANY ORGANIZATIONS involved?**

(tracking orgs/groups can add important details to college applications + possibly lead to future scholarship opportunities related to certain groups)

**YOUR POSITION or leadership role?**

(past roles can reveal growth over time...like event planner, class rep, club leader, part-time job title, sports position, project leader, mentor etc)

**HOURS spent per WEEK:**

(this is required on most college applications so start tracking early... hours do NOT have to be exact, can be an average)

**KEY NUMBERS to remember?**

(data points add great context to a story...like how many people you helped, how many club members you led, how many event attendees, total $ funds raised, etc)

**Special ADVOCATES to remember?**

(your past supporters can someday turn into valuable Letters of Recommendation... for college, awards, and scholarships!)

**INSERT** any special documents between these two Story pages to create a convenient folder (photos, awards, thank you notes, event flyers, email printouts etc...also sticky notes with more details!)

# STORY NOTES - What happened?

Were you creative in some way?  Did you solve a problem?  Did you impact others in a positive way?
Did you practice leadership?  How did you grow or learn from this?  Anything else to remember?
(your personal insights + noteworthy data points can lead to amazing future college essays)

# GROWTH STORY  # 25

Answer any questions **relevant** to this story – **you do not have to fill in every box.**

**SHORT**
title or
keywords:

(for easy reference later
when looking back on
your special moments)

**DATES**
to remember?

☐ School **YEAR**

☐ School **BREAK**

**ANY**
ORGANIZATIONS
involved?

(tracking orgs/groups
can add important details
to college applications
+ possibly lead to future
scholarship opportunities
related to certain groups)

**YOUR**
POSITION
or leadership
role?

(past roles can reveal
growth over time...like
event planner, class rep,
club leader, part-time
job title, sports position,
project leader, mentor etc)

**HOURS** spent
per **WEEK:**

(this is required on most
college applications
so start tracking early...
hours do NOT have to be
exact, can be an average)

**KEY**
NUMBERS
to remember?

(data points add great
context to a story...like
how many people you
helped, how many club
members you led, how
many event attendees,
total $ funds raised, etc)

Special
**ADVOCATES**
to remember?

(your past supporters
can someday turn into
valuable Letters of
Recommendation...
for college, awards,
and scholarships!)

**Keepsakes Folder!**

**56**

**INSERT** any special documents between these two Story pages
to create a convenient folder (photos, awards, thank you notes,
event flyers, email printouts etc...also sticky notes with more details!)

## STORY NOTES - What happened?

Were you creative in some way?  Did you solve a problem?  Did you impact others in a positive way?
Did you practice leadership?  How did you grow or learn from this?  Anything else to remember?
(your personal insights + noteworthy data points can lead to amazing future college essays)

# GROWTH STORY # 26

Answer any questions **relevant** to this story – **you do not have to fill in every box.**

**SHORT title or keywords:**

(for easy reference later when looking back on your special moments)

**DATES to remember?**

☐ School **YEAR**

☐ School **BREAK**

**ANY ORGANIZATIONS involved?**

(tracking orgs/groups can add important details to college applications + possibly lead to future scholarship opportunities related to certain groups)

**YOUR POSITION or leadership role?**

(past roles can reveal growth over time...like event planner, class rep, club leader, part-time job title, sports position, project leader, mentor etc)

**HOURS spent per WEEK:**

(this is required on most college applications so start tracking early... hours do NOT have to be exact, can be an average)

**KEY NUMBERS to remember?**

(data points add great context to a story...like how many people you helped, how many club members you led, how many event attendees, total $ funds raised, etc)

**Special ADVOCATES to remember?**

(your past supporters can someday turn into valuable Letters of Recommendation... for college, awards, and scholarships!)

 **Keepsakes Folder!**

**INSERT** any special documents between these two Story pages to create a convenient folder (photos, awards, thank you notes, event flyers, email printouts etc...also sticky notes with more details!)

# STORY NOTES - What happened?

Were you creative in some way?  Did you solve a problem?  Did you impact others in a positive way?
Did you practice leadership?  How did you grow or learn from this?  Anything else to remember?
(your personal insights + noteworthy data points can lead to amazing future college essays)

# GROWTH STORY # 27

Answer any questions **relevant** to this story – **you do not have to fill in every box.**

**SHORT** title or keywords:

(for easy reference later when looking back on your special moments)

**DATES** to remember?

☐ School **YEAR**

☐ School **BREAK**

**ANY ORGANIZATIONS** involved?

(tracking orgs/groups can add important details to college applications + possibly lead to future scholarship opportunities related to certain groups)

**YOUR POSITION** or leadership role?

(past roles can reveal growth over time...like event planner, class rep, club leader, part-time job title, sports position, project leader, mentor etc)

**HOURS** spent per **WEEK:**

(this is required on most college applications so start tracking early... hours do NOT have to be exact, can be an average)

**KEY NUMBERS** to remember?

(data points add great context to a story...like how many people you helped, how many club members you led, how many event attendees, total $ funds raised, etc)

Special **ADVOCATES** to remember?

(your past supporters can someday turn into valuable Letters of Recommendation... for college, awards, and scholarships!)

## Keepsakes Folder!

**INSERT** any special documents between these two Story pages to create a convenient folder (photos, awards, thank you notes, event flyers, email printouts etc...also sticky notes with more details!)

# STORY NOTES - What happened?

Were you creative in some way?  Did you solve a problem?  Did you impact others in a positive way?
Did you practice leadership?  How did you grow or learn from this?  Anything else to remember?
(your personal insights + noteworthy data points can lead to amazing future college essays)

# GROWTH STORY # 28

Answer any questions **relevant** to this story – **you do not have to fill in every box.**

**SHORT**
title or
keywords:

(for easy reference later
when looking back on
your special moments)

**DATES**
to remember?

☐ School **YEAR**

☐ School **BREAK**

**ANY**
ORGANIZATIONS
involved?

(tracking orgs/groups
can add important details
to college applications
+ possibly lead to future
scholarship opportunities
related to certain groups)

**YOUR**
POSITION
or leadership
role?

(past roles can reveal
growth over time...like
event planner, class rep,
club leader, part-time
job title, sports position,
project leader, mentor etc)

HOURS spent
per WEEK:

(this is required on most
college applications
so start tracking early...
hours do NOT have to be
exact, can be an average)

**KEY**
NUMBERS
to remember?

(data points add great
context to a story...like
how many people you
helped, how many club
members you led, how
many event attendees,
total $ funds raised, etc)

Special
ADVOCATES
to remember?

(your past supporters
can someday turn into
valuable Letters of
Recommendation...
for college, awards,
and scholarships!)

# Keepsakes
## Folder!

62

**INSERT** any special documents between these two Story pages
to create a convenient folder (photos, awards, thank you notes,
event flyers, email printouts etc...also sticky notes with more details!)

# STORY NOTES - What happened?

Were you creative in some way?  Did you solve a problem?  Did you impact others in a positive way?
Did you practice leadership?  How did you grow or learn from this?  Anything else to remember?
(your personal insights + noteworthy data points can lead to amazing future college essays)

# GROWTH STORY # 29

Answer any questions **relevant** to this story – **you do not have to fill in every box.**

**SHORT** title or keywords:

(for easy reference later when looking back on your special moments)

**DATES** to remember?

☐ School **YEAR**

☐ School **BREAK**

**ANY ORGANIZATIONS** involved?

(tracking orgs/groups can add important details to college applications + possibly lead to future scholarship opportunities related to certain groups)

**YOUR POSITION** or leadership role?

(past roles can reveal growth over time...like event planner, class rep, club leader, part-time job title, sports position, project leader, mentor etc)

**HOURS** spent per **WEEK:**

(this is required on most college applications so start tracking early... hours do NOT have to be exact, can be an average)

**KEY NUMBERS** to remember?

(data points add great context to a story...like how many people you helped, how many club members you led, how many event attendees, total $ funds raised, etc)

Special **ADVOCATES** to remember?

(your past supporters can someday turn into valuable Letters of Recommendation... for college, awards, and scholarships!)

# Keepsakes Folder!

**INSERT** any special documents between these two Story pages to create a convenient folder (photos, awards, thank you notes, event flyers, email printouts etc...also sticky notes with more details!)

# STORY NOTES - What happened?

Were you creative in some way?  Did you solve a problem?  Did you impact others in a positive way?
Did you practice leadership?  How did you grow or learn from this?  Anything else to remember?
(your personal insights + noteworthy data points can lead to amazing future college essays)

# GROWTH STORY # 30

Answer any questions **relevant** to this story – **you do not have to fill in every box.**

**SHORT** title or keywords:

(for easy reference later when looking back on your special moments)

**DATES** to remember?

☐ School **YEAR**

☐ School **BREAK**

**ANY ORGANIZATIONS** involved?

(tracking orgs/groups can add important details to college applications + possibly lead to future scholarship opportunities related to certain groups)

**YOUR POSITION** or leadership role?

(past roles can reveal growth over time...like event planner, class rep, club leader, part-time job title, sports position, project leader, mentor etc)

**HOURS** spent per **WEEK:**

(this is required on most college applications so start tracking early... hours do NOT have to be exact, can be an average)

**KEY NUMBERS** to remember?

(data points add great context to a story...like how many people you helped, how many club members you led, how many event attendees, total $ funds raised, etc)

Special **ADVOCATES** to remember?

(your past supporters can someday turn into valuable Letters of Recommendation... for college, awards, and scholarships!)

**Keepsakes Folder!**

**INSERT** any special documents between these two Story pages to create a convenient folder (photos, awards, thank you notes, event flyers, email printouts etc...also sticky notes with more details!)

# STORY NOTES - What happened?

Were you creative in some way?  Did you solve a problem?  Did you impact others in a positive way?
Did you practice leadership?  How did you grow or learn from this?  Anything else to remember?
(your personal insights + noteworthy data points can lead to amazing future college essays)

# GROWTH STORY  # 31

Answer any questions **relevant** to this story — **you do not have to fill in every box.**

**SHORT** title or keywords:

(for easy reference later when looking back on your special moments)

**DATES** to remember?

☐ School **YEAR**

☐ School **BREAK**

**ANY ORGANIZATIONS** involved?

(tracking orgs/groups can add important details to college applications + possibly lead to future scholarship opportunities related to certain groups)

**YOUR POSITION** or leadership role?

(past roles can reveal growth over time...like event planner, class rep, club leader, part-time job title, sports position, project leader, mentor etc)

**HOURS spent** per **WEEK:**

(this is required on most college applications so start tracking early... hours do NOT have to be exact, can be an average)

**KEY NUMBERS** to remember?

(data points add great context to a story...like how many people you helped, how many club members you led, how many event attendees, total $ funds raised, etc)

Special **ADVOCATES** to remember?

(your past supporters can someday turn into valuable Letters of Recommendation... for college, awards, and scholarships!)

# Keepsakes Folder!

**68**

**INSERT** any special documents between these two Story pages to create a convenient folder (photos, awards, thank you notes, event flyers, email printouts etc...also sticky notes with more details!)

# STORY NOTES - What happened?

Were you creative in some way?  Did you solve a problem?  Did you impact others in a positive way?
Did you practice leadership?  How did you grow or learn from this?  Anything else to remember?
(your personal insights + noteworthy data points can lead to amazing future college essays)

# GROWTH STORY # 32

Answer any questions **relevant** to this story – **you do not have to fill in every box.**

**SHORT title or keywords:**
(for easy reference later when looking back on your special moments)

**DATES to remember?**
☐ School **YEAR**
☐ School **BREAK**

**ANY ORGANIZATIONS involved?**
(tracking orgs/groups can add important details to college applications + possibly lead to future scholarship opportunities related to certain groups)

**YOUR POSITION or leadership role?**
(past roles can reveal growth over time...like event planner, class rep, club leader, part-time job title, sports position, project leader, mentor etc)

**HOURS spent per WEEK:**
(this is required on most college applications so start tracking early... hours do NOT have to be exact, can be an average)

**KEY NUMBERS to remember?**
(data points add great context to a story...like how many people you helped, how many club members you led, how many event attendees, total $ funds raised, etc)

**Special ADVOCATES to remember?**
(your past supporters can someday turn into valuable Letters of Recommendation... for college, awards, and scholarships!)

**Keepsakes Folder!**

**INSERT** any special documents between these two Story pages to create a convenient folder (photos, awards, thank you notes, event flyers, email printouts etc...also sticky notes with more details!)

## STORY NOTES - What happened?

Were you creative in some way?  Did you solve a problem?  Did you impact others in a positive way?
Did you practice leadership?  How did you grow or learn from this?  Anything else to remember?
(your personal insights + noteworthy data points can lead to amazing future college essays)

# GROWTH STORY # 33

Answer any questions **relevant** to this story — **you do not have to fill in every box.**

**SHORT** title or keywords:

(for easy reference later when looking back on your special moments)

**DATES** to remember?

☐ School **YEAR**

☐ School **BREAK**

**ANY ORGANIZATIONS** involved?

(tracking orgs/groups can add important details to college applications + possibly lead to future scholarship opportunities related to certain groups)

**YOUR POSITION** or leadership role?

(past roles can reveal growth over time...like event planner, class rep, club leader, part-time job title, sports position, project leader, mentor etc)

**HOURS** spent per **WEEK:**

(this is required on most college applications so start tracking early... hours do NOT have to be exact, can be an average)

**KEY NUMBERS** to remember?

(data points add great context to a story...like how many people you helped, how many club members you led, how many event attendees, total $ funds raised, etc)

Special **ADVOCATES** to remember?

(your past supporters can someday turn into valuable Letters of Recommendation... for college, awards, and scholarships!)

# Keepsakes Folder!

**INSERT** any special documents between these two Story pages to create a convenient folder (photos, awards, thank you notes, event flyers, email printouts etc...also sticky notes with more details!)

# STORY NOTES - What happened?

Were you creative in some way?  Did you solve a problem?  Did you impact others in a positive way?
Did you practice leadership?  How did you grow or learn from this?  Anything else to remember?
(your personal insights + noteworthy data points can lead to amazing future college essays)

# GROWTH STORY  # 34

Answer any questions **relevant** to this story – **you do not have to fill in every box.**

**SHORT** title or keywords:

(for easy reference later when looking back on your special moments)

**DATES** to remember?

☐ School **YEAR**

☐ School **BREAK**

**ANY ORGANIZATIONS** involved?

(tracking orgs/groups can add important details to college applications + possibly lead to future scholarship opportunities related to certain groups)

**YOUR POSITION** or leadership role?

(past roles can reveal growth over time...like event planner, class rep, club leader, part-time job title, sports position, project leader, mentor etc)

**HOURS** spent per **WEEK**:

(this is required on most college applications so start tracking early... hours do NOT have to be exact, can be an average)

**KEY NUMBERS** to remember?

(data points add great context to a story...like how many people you helped, how many club members you led, how many event attendees, total $ funds raised, etc)

Special **ADVOCATES** to remember?

(your past supporters can someday turn into valuable Letters of Recommendation... for college, awards, and scholarships!)

**Keepsakes Folder!**

**INSERT** any special documents between these two Story pages to create a convenient folder (photos, awards, thank you notes, event flyers, email printouts etc...also sticky notes with more details!)

# STORY NOTES - What happened?

Were you creative in some way?  Did you solve a problem?  Did you impact others in a positive way?
Did you practice leadership?  How did you grow or learn from this?  Anything else to remember?
(your personal insights + noteworthy data points can lead to amazing future college essays)

# GROWTH STORY # 35

Answer any questions **relevant** to this story – **you do not have to fill in every box.**

**SHORT title or keywords:**

(for easy reference later when looking back on your special moments)

**DATES to remember?**

☐ School **YEAR**

☐ School **BREAK**

**ANY ORGANIZATIONS involved?**

(tracking orgs/groups can add important details to college applications + possibly lead to future scholarship opportunities related to certain groups)

**YOUR POSITION or leadership role?**

(past roles can reveal growth over time...like event planner, class rep, club leader, part-time job title, sports position, project leader, mentor etc)

**HOURS spent per WEEK:**

(this is required on most college applications so start tracking early... hours do NOT have to be exact, can be an average)

**KEY NUMBERS to remember?**

(data points add great context to a story...like how many people you helped, how many club members you led, how many event attendees, total $ funds raised, etc)

**Special ADVOCATES to remember?**

(your past supporters can someday turn into valuable Letters of Recommendation... for college, awards, and scholarships!)

**Keepsakes Folder!**

**INSERT** any special documents between these two Story pages to create a convenient folder (photos, awards, thank you notes, event flyers, email printouts etc...also sticky notes with more details!)

# STORY NOTES - What happened?

Were you creative in some way?  Did you solve a problem?  Did you impact others in a positive way?
Did you practice leadership?  How did you grow or learn from this?  Anything else to remember?
(your personal insights + noteworthy data points can lead to amazing future college essays)

# GROWTH STORY # 36

Answer any questions **relevant** to this story – **you do not have to fill in every box.**

**SHORT** title or keywords:

(for easy reference later when looking back on your special moments)

**DATES** to remember?

☐ School **YEAR**

☐ School **BREAK**

**ANY ORGANIZATIONS** involved?

(tracking orgs/groups can add important details to college applications + possibly lead to future scholarship opportunities related to certain groups)

**YOUR POSITION** or leadership role?

(past roles can reveal growth over time...like event planner, class rep, club leader, part-time job title, sports position, project leader, mentor etc)

**HOURS** spent per **WEEK:**

(this is required on most college applications so start tracking early... hours do NOT have to be exact, can be an average)

**KEY NUMBERS** to remember?

(data points add great context to a story...like how many people you helped, how many club members you led, how many event attendees, total $ funds raised, etc)

Special **ADVOCATES** to remember?

(your past supporters can someday turn into valuable Letters of Recommendation... for college, awards, and scholarships!)

## Keepsakes Folder!

78

**INSERT** any special documents between these two Story pages to create a convenient folder (photos, awards, thank you notes, event flyers, email printouts etc...also sticky notes with more details!)

# STORY NOTES - What happened?

Were you creative in some way?  Did you solve a problem?  Did you impact others in a positive way?
Did you practice leadership?  How did you grow or learn from this?  Anything else to remember?
(your personal insights + noteworthy data points can lead to amazing future college essays)

# GROWTH STORY  # 37

Answer any questions **relevant** to this story — **you do not have to fill in every box.**

**SHORT** title or keywords:

(for easy reference later when looking back on your special moments)

**DATES** to remember?

☐ School **YEAR**

☐ School **BREAK**

**ANY ORGANIZATIONS** involved?

(tracking orgs/groups can add important details to college applications + possibly lead to future scholarship opportunities related to certain groups)

**YOUR POSITION** or leadership role?

(past roles can reveal growth over time...like event planner, class rep, club leader, part-time job title, sports position, project leader, mentor etc)

**HOURS spent** per **WEEK:**

(this is required on most college applications so start tracking early... hours do NOT have to be exact, can be an average)

**KEY NUMBERS** to remember?

(data points add great context to a story...like how many people you helped, how many club members you led, how many event attendees, total $ funds raised, etc)

Special **ADVOCATES** to remember?

(your past supporters can someday turn into valuable Letters of Recommendation... for college, awards, and scholarships!)

**Keepsakes Folder!**

80

**INSERT** any special documents between these two Story pages to create a convenient folder (photos, awards, thank you notes, event flyers, email printouts etc...also sticky notes with more details!)

## STORY NOTES - What happened?

Were you creative in some way?  Did you solve a problem?  Did you impact others in a positive way?
Did you practice leadership?  How did you grow or learn from this?  Anything else to remember?
(your personal insights + noteworthy data points can lead to amazing future college essays)

# GROWTH STORY # 38

Answer any questions **relevant** to this story – **you do not have to fill in every box.**

**SHORT** title or keywords:

(for easy reference later when looking back on your special moments)

**DATES** to remember?

☐ School **YEAR**

☐ School **BREAK**

**ANY ORGANIZATIONS** involved?

(tracking orgs/groups can add important details to college applications + possibly lead to future scholarship opportunities related to certain groups)

**YOUR POSITION** or leadership role?

(past roles can reveal growth over time...like event planner, class rep, club leader, part-time job title, sports position, project leader, mentor etc)

**HOURS** spent per **WEEK:**

(this is required on most college applications so start tracking early... hours do NOT have to be exact, can be an average)

**KEY NUMBERS** to remember?

(data points add great context to a story...like how many people you helped, how many club members you led, how many event attendees, total $ funds raised, etc)

Special **ADVOCATES** to remember?

(your past supporters can someday turn into valuable Letters of Recommendation... for college, awards, and scholarships!)

# Keepsakes
## Folder!

**INSERT** any special documents between these two Story pages to create a convenient folder (photos, awards, thank you notes, event flyers, email printouts etc...also sticky notes with more details!)

## STORY NOTES - What happened?

Were you creative in some way?  Did you solve a problem?  Did you impact others in a positive way?
Did you practice leadership?  How did you grow or learn from this?  Anything else to remember?
(your personal insights + noteworthy data points can lead to amazing future college essays)

# GROWTH STORY  # 39

Answer any questions **relevant** to this story – **you do not have to fill in every box.**

**SHORT** title or keywords:

(for easy reference later when looking back on your special moments)

**DATES** to remember?

☐ School **YEAR**

☐ School **BREAK**

**ANY ORGANIZATIONS** involved?

(tracking orgs/groups can add important details to college applications + possibly lead to future scholarship opportunities related to certain groups)

**YOUR POSITION** or leadership role?

(past roles can reveal growth over time...like event planner, class rep, club leader, part-time job title, sports position, project leader, mentor etc)

**HOURS** spent per **WEEK**:

(this is required on most college applications so start tracking early... hours do NOT have to be exact, can be an average)

**KEY NUMBERS** to remember?

(data points add great context to a story...like how many people you helped, how many club members you led, how many event attendees, total $ funds raised, etc)

Special **ADVOCATES** to remember?

(your past supporters can someday turn into valuable Letters of Recommendation... for college, awards, and scholarships!)

# Keepsakes Folder!

84

**INSERT** any special documents between these two Story pages to create a convenient folder (photos, awards, thank you notes, event flyers, email printouts etc...also sticky notes with more details!)

# STORY NOTES - What happened?

Were you creative in some way?  Did you solve a problem?  Did you impact others in a positive way?
Did you practice leadership?  How did you grow or learn from this?  Anything else to remember?
(your personal insights + noteworthy data points can lead to amazing future college essays)

# GROWTH STORY  # 40

Answer any questions **relevant** to this story – **you do not have to fill in every box.**

**SHORT**
title or
keywords:

(for easy reference later
when looking back on
your special moments)

**DATES**
to remember?

☐ School **YEAR**

☐ School **BREAK**

**ANY**
**ORGANIZATIONS**
involved?

(tracking orgs/groups
can add important details
to college applications
+ possibly lead to future
scholarship opportunities
related to certain groups)

**YOUR**
**POSITION**
or leadership
role?

(past roles can reveal
growth over time...like
event planner, class rep,
club leader, part-time
job title, sports position,
project leader, mentor etc)

**HOURS** spent
per **WEEK:**

(this is required on most
college applications
so start tracking early...
hours do NOT have to be
exact, can be an average)

**KEY**
**NUMBERS**
to remember?

(data points add great
context to a story...like
how many people you
helped, how many club
members you led, how
many event attendees,
total $ funds raised, etc)

Special
**ADVOCATES**
to remember?

(your past supporters
can someday turn into
valuable Letters of
Recommendation...
for college, awards,
and scholarships!)

# Keepsakes
# Folder!

**86**

**INSERT** any special documents between these two Story pages
to create a convenient folder (photos, awards, thank you notes,
event flyers, email printouts etc...also sticky notes with more details!)

# STORY NOTES - What happened?

Were you creative in some way?  Did you solve a problem?  Did you impact others in a positive way?
Did you practice leadership?  How did you grow or learn from this?  Anything else to remember?
(your personal insights + noteworthy data points can lead to amazing future college essays)

# GROWTH STORY # 41

Answer any questions **relevant** to this story – **you do not have to fill in every box.**

**SHORT** title or keywords:

(for easy reference later when looking back on your special moments)

**DATES** to remember?

☐ School **YEAR**

☐ School **BREAK**

**ANY ORGANIZATIONS** involved?

(tracking orgs/groups can add important details to college applications + possibly lead to future scholarship opportunities related to certain groups)

**YOUR POSITION** or leadership role?

(past roles can reveal growth over time...like event planner, class rep, club leader, part-time job title, sports position, project leader, mentor etc)

**HOURS** spent per **WEEK:**

(this is required on most college applications so start tracking early... hours do NOT have to be exact, can be an average)

**KEY NUMBERS** to remember?

(data points add great context to a story...like how many people you helped, how many club members you led, how many event attendees, total $ funds raised, etc)

Special **ADVOCATES** to remember?

(your past supporters can someday turn into valuable Letters of Recommendation... for college, awards, and scholarships!)

# Keepsakes Folder!

**INSERT** any special documents between these two Story pages to create a convenient folder (photos, awards, thank you notes, event flyers, email printouts etc...also sticky notes with more details!)

## STORY NOTES - What happened?

Were you creative in some way?  Did you solve a problem?  Did you impact others in a positive way?
Did you practice leadership?  How did you grow or learn from this?  Anything else to remember?
(your personal insights + noteworthy data points can lead to amazing future college essays)

# GROWTH STORY # 42

Answer any questions **relevant** to this story – **you do not have to fill in every box.**

**SHORT title or keywords:**

(for easy reference later when looking back on your special moments)

**DATES to remember?**

☐ School **YEAR**

☐ School **BREAK**

**ANY ORGANIZATIONS involved?**

(tracking orgs/groups can add important details to college applications + possibly lead to future scholarship opportunities related to certain groups)

**YOUR POSITION or leadership role?**

(past roles can reveal growth over time...like event planner, class rep, club leader, part-time job title, sports position, project leader, mentor etc)

**HOURS spent per WEEK:**

(this is required on most college applications so start tracking early... hours do NOT have to be exact, can be an average)

**KEY NUMBERS to remember?**

(data points add great context to a story...like how many people you helped, how many club members you led, how many event attendees, total $ funds raised, etc)

**Special ADVOCATES to remember?**

(your past supporters can someday turn into valuable Letters of Recommendation... for college, awards, and scholarships!)

**Keepsakes Folder!**

**INSERT** any special documents between these two Story pages to create a convenient folder (photos, awards, thank you notes, event flyers, email printouts etc...also sticky notes with more details!)

# STORY NOTES - What happened?

Were you creative in some way?  Did you solve a problem?  Did you impact others in a positive way?
Did you practice leadership?  How did you grow or learn from this?  Anything else to remember?
(your personal insights + noteworthy data points can lead to amazing future college essays)

# GROWTH STORY #43

Answer any questions **relevant** to this story – **you do not have to fill in every box.**

**SHORT** title or keywords:

(for easy reference later when looking back on your special moments)

**DATES** to remember?

☐ School **YEAR**

☐ School **BREAK**

**ANY ORGANIZATIONS** involved?

(tracking orgs/groups can add important details to college applications + possibly lead to future scholarship opportunities related to certain groups)

**YOUR POSITION** or leadership role?

(past roles can reveal growth over time...like event planner, class rep, club leader, part-time job title, sports position, project leader, mentor etc)

**HOURS** spent per **WEEK:**

(this is required on most college applications so start tracking early... hours do NOT have to be exact, can be an average)

**KEY NUMBERS** to remember?

(data points add great context to a story...like how many people you helped, how many club members you led, how many event attendees, total $ funds raised, etc)

Special **ADVOCATES** to remember?

(your past supporters can someday turn into valuable Letters of Recommendation... for college, awards, and scholarships!)

**Keepsakes Folder!**

**INSERT** any special documents between these two Story pages to create a convenient folder (photos, awards, thank you notes, event flyers, email printouts etc...also sticky notes with more details!)

# STORY NOTES - What happened?

Were you creative in some way?  Did you solve a problem?  Did you impact others in a positive way?
Did you practice leadership?  How did you grow or learn from this?  Anything else to remember?
(your personal insights + noteworthy data points can lead to amazing future college essays)

# GROWTH STORY # 44

Answer any questions **relevant** to this story – **you do not have to fill in every box.**

**SHORT** title or keywords:

(for easy reference later when looking back on your special moments)

**DATES** to remember?

☐ School **YEAR**

☐ School **BREAK**

**ANY ORGANIZATIONS** involved?

(tracking orgs/groups can add important details to college applications + possibly lead to future scholarship opportunities related to certain groups)

**YOUR POSITION** or leadership role?

(past roles can reveal growth over time...like event planner, class rep, club leader, part-time job title, sports position, project leader, mentor etc)

**HOURS** spent per **WEEK:**

(this is required on most college applications so start tracking early... hours do NOT have to be exact, can be an average)

**KEY NUMBERS** to remember?

(data points add great context to a story...like how many people you helped, how many club members you led, how many event attendees, total $ funds raised, etc)

Special **ADVOCATES** to remember?

(your past supporters can someday turn into valuable Letters of Recommendation... for college, awards, and scholarships!)

## Keepsakes Folder!

94

**INSERT** any special documents between these two Story pages to create a convenient folder (photos, awards, thank you notes, event flyers, email printouts etc...also sticky notes with more details!)

## STORY NOTES - What happened?

Were you creative in some way?  Did you solve a problem?  Did you impact others in a positive way?
Did you practice leadership?  How did you grow or learn from this?  Anything else to remember?
(your personal insights + noteworthy data points can lead to amazing future college essays)

# GROWTH STORY # 45

Answer any questions **relevant** to this story – **you do not have to fill in every box.**

**SHORT** title or keywords:

(for easy reference later when looking back on your special moments)

**DATES** to remember?

☐ School **YEAR**

☐ School **BREAK**

**ANY ORGANIZATIONS** involved?

(tracking orgs/groups can add important details to college applications + possibly lead to future scholarship opportunities related to certain groups)

**YOUR POSITION** or leadership role?

(past roles can reveal growth over time...like event planner, class rep, club leader, part-time job title, sports position, project leader, mentor etc)

**HOURS** spent per **WEEK:**

(this is required on most college applications so start tracking early... hours do NOT have to be exact, can be an average)

**KEY NUMBERS** to remember?

(data points add great context to a story...like how many people you helped, how many club members you led, how many event attendees, total $ funds raised, etc)

Special **ADVOCATES** to remember?

(your past supporters can someday turn into valuable Letters of Recommendation... for college, awards, and scholarships!)

## Keepsakes Folder!

**INSERT** any special documents between these two Story pages to create a convenient folder (photos, awards, thank you notes, event flyers, email printouts etc...also sticky notes with more details!)

# STORY NOTES - What happened?

Were you creative in some way?  Did you solve a problem?  Did you impact others in a positive way?
Did you practice leadership?  How did you grow or learn from this?  Anything else to remember?
(your personal insights + noteworthy data points can lead to amazing future college essays)

# GROWTH STORY # 46

Answer any questions **relevant** to this story – **you do not have to fill in every box.**

**SHORT title or keywords:**

(for easy reference later when looking back on your special moments)

**DATES to remember?**

☐ School **YEAR**

☐ School **BREAK**

**ANY ORGANIZATIONS involved?**

(tracking orgs/groups can add important details to college applications + possibly lead to future scholarship opportunities related to certain groups)

**YOUR POSITION or leadership role?**

(past roles can reveal growth over time...like event planner, class rep, club leader, part-time job title, sports position, project leader, mentor etc)

**HOURS spent per WEEK:**

(this is required on most college applications so start tracking early... hours do NOT have to be exact, can be an average)

**KEY NUMBERS to remember?**

(data points add great context to a story...like how many people you helped, how many club members you led, how many event attendees, total $ funds raised, etc)

**Special ADVOCATES to remember?**

(your past supporters can someday turn into valuable Letters of Recommendation... for college, awards, and scholarships!)

## Keepsakes Folder!

**INSERT** any special documents between these two Story pages to create a convenient folder (photos, awards, thank you notes, event flyers, email printouts etc...also sticky notes with more details!)

# STORY NOTES - What happened?

Were you creative in some way?  Did you solve a problem?  Did you impact others in a positive way?
Did you practice leadership?  How did you grow or learn from this?  Anything else to remember?
(your personal insights + noteworthy data points can lead to amazing future college essays)

# GROWTH STORY  # 47

Answer any questions **relevant** to this story – **you do not have to fill in every box.**

**SHORT** title or keywords:

(for easy reference later when looking back on your special moments)

**DATES** to remember?

☐ School **YEAR**

☐ School **BREAK**

**ANY ORGANIZATIONS** involved?

(tracking orgs/groups can add important details to college applications + possibly lead to future scholarship opportunities related to certain groups)

**YOUR POSITION** or leadership role?

(past roles can reveal growth over time...like event planner, class rep, club leader, part-time job title, sports position, project leader, mentor etc)

**HOURS** spent per **WEEK:**

(this is required on most college applications so start tracking early... hours do NOT have to be exact, can be an average)

**KEY NUMBERS** to remember?

(data points add great context to a story...like how many people you helped, how many club members you led, how many event attendees, total $ funds raised, etc)

Special **ADVOCATES** to remember?

(your past supporters can someday turn into valuable Letters of Recommendation... for college, awards, and scholarships!)

# Keepsakes Folder!

100

**INSERT** any special documents between these two Story pages to create a convenient folder (photos, awards, thank you notes, event flyers, email printouts etc...also sticky notes with more details!)

# STORY NOTES - What happened?

Were you creative in some way?  Did you solve a problem?  Did you impact others in a positive way?
Did you practice leadership?  How did you grow or learn from this?  Anything else to remember?
(your personal insights + noteworthy data points can lead to amazing future college essays)

# GROWTH STORY # 48

Answer any questions **relevant** to this story – **you do not have to fill in every box.**

**SHORT**
title or
keywords:

(for easy reference later
when looking back on
your special moments)

**DATES**
to remember?

☐ School **YEAR**

☐ School **BREAK**

**ANY**
ORGANIZATIONS
involved?

(tracking orgs/groups
can add important details
to college applications
+ possibly lead to future
scholarship opportunities
related to certain groups)

**YOUR**
POSITION
or leadership
role?

(past roles can reveal
growth over time...like
event planner, class rep,
club leader, part-time
job title, sports position,
project leader, mentor etc)

HOURS spent
per WEEK:

(this is required on most
college applications
so start tracking early...
hours do NOT have to be
exact, can be an average)

**KEY**
NUMBERS
to remember?

(data points add great
context to a story...like
how many people you
helped, how many club
members you led, how
many event attendees,
total $ funds raised, etc)

Special
ADVOCATES
to remember?

(your past supporters
can someday turn into
valuable Letters of
Recommendation...
for college, awards,
and scholarships!)

# Keepsakes
# Folder!

**INSERT** any special documents between these two Story pages
to create a convenient folder (photos, awards, thank you notes,
event flyers, email printouts etc...also sticky notes with more details!)

# STORY NOTES - What happened?

Were you creative in some way?  Did you solve a problem?  Did you impact others in a positive way?
Did you practice leadership?  How did you grow or learn from this?  Anything else to remember?
(your personal insights + noteworthy data points can lead to amazing future college essays)

# GROWTH STORY # 49

Answer any questions **relevant** to this story – **you do not have to fill in every box.**

**SHORT** title or keywords:

(for easy reference later when looking back on your special moments)

**DATES** to remember?

☐ School **YEAR**

☐ School **BREAK**

**ANY ORGANIZATIONS** involved?

(tracking orgs/groups can add important details to college applications + possibly lead to future scholarship opportunities related to certain groups)

**YOUR POSITION** or leadership role?

(past roles can reveal growth over time...like event planner, class rep, club leader, part-time job title, sports position, project leader, mentor etc)

**HOURS** spent per **WEEK**:

(this is required on most college applications so start tracking early... hours do NOT have to be exact, can be an average)

**KEY NUMBERS** to remember?

(data points add great context to a story...like how many people you helped, how many club members you led, how many event attendees, total $ funds raised, etc)

Special **ADVOCATES** to remember?

(your past supporters can someday turn into valuable Letters of Recommendation... for college, awards, and scholarships!)

# Keepsakes Folder!

104

**INSERT** any special documents between these two Story pages to create a convenient folder (photos, awards, thank you notes, event flyers, email printouts etc...also sticky notes with more details!)

# STORY NOTES - What happened?

Were you creative in some way?  Did you solve a problem?  Did you impact others in a positive way? Did you practice leadership?  How did you grow or learn from this?  Anything else to remember? (your personal insights + noteworthy data points can lead to amazing future college essays)

# 8 Insider Tips (to know EARLY)

### 1. Keep a LOG (this guided book is the perfect start)

Keeping track of anything noteworthy over the years makes college applications so much easier. Start now – make note of any personal wins, problems solved, key lessons learned, growth experiences and data points.

### 2. Think WIN-WIN

A win-win mindset means you seek to boost others as you grow & succeed. Another way to put this – develop a superpower, and use it for good.

How can you do this? Grow your special talents, then share them! Share by tackling a real problem in the community (go for social impact).

### 3. LEAD something + leave your mark

Colleges like to see initiative. Admissions officers look for evidence of future leaders, innovative thinkers & change makers – they find this evidence by evaluating past activities and carefully reviewing essays.

### 4. Find ADVOCATES

Past supporters can one day turn into valuable Letters of Recommendation for college admission, awards and scholarships.

Advocates are people who KNOW & LIKE you – and who can speak to your growth through past experiences or stories. These are often teachers, mentors, coaches etc. No fancy titles needed (but generally no family).

*Letters of Recommendation can tip the scale in your college applications.*

## 5. Seek DIVERSITY

Work or volunteer with others who don't look like you.
Remember – diversity is not only ethnic or racial differences,
but can include differences in thoughts and talents too.

Top colleges care about diversity and seek students with an
appreciation for different people, backgrounds and perspectives.

## 6. Nurture a love for LEARNING (for the sake of learning)

Be curious. Develop a thirst for knowledge. Seek out opportunities
to learn OUTSIDE of school. Colleges look for students who pursue
learning both IN & OUT of their classrooms. Some essay questions
are specifically crafted to assess your level of "intellectual curiosity".

## 7. Preview ESSAY QUESTIONS now

Don't be surprised by college essay questions when the time comes!
These essays are a window into who you are – AND what matters to you.
Essay prep is critical because personal narratives can **heavily tip the
scale** toward success in your college applications (and scholarships).

See common college Essay Questions on the NEXT PAGES...

## 8. Above all else – Be KIND

Be a nice person, no matter how ambitious you are.

Yes, school can be very stressful...
but there is ALWAYS room for kindness and compassion.

The ideal incoming college freshman is both **smart & kind**. Dorms,
classes and college life are more enjoyable and harmonious when the
campus is kind. Admissions officers can often sense this hidden kindness
factor in your essays. Letters of recommendation writers often comment
on kindness characteristics when sharing their past impressions of you...

**This tip is more important than you think!!**

# Essay Questions

Preview today's college essay questions
(*avoid surprises later!*)

## The "Common App"

Approx. 1000 colleges use the "Common App" application (U.S. + international).

The Common App essay is the main personal statement you'll submit to these colleges. This big essay is a chance to tell your story – growth, interests, strengths, experiences, skills, etc.  Students choose 1 of 7 essay prompts.

**Important:**  In addition to the Common App essay, many colleges **ALSO** require supplemental essays (each campus website lists their additional essay questions).

### Essay Questions to preview – based on the Common App:

1. Share your story if you have a background, identity, interest, or talent especially meaningful that it completes your application.

2. Write about a time you faced an obstacle, challenge, setback, or failure. Share how it affected you, what you learned, etc.

3. Write about a time you questioned an idea or belief. Share what led to this and describe the outcome.

4. Write about a time someone did something for you that surprisingly made you thankful or happy. Share how your gratitude has motivated you.

5. Write about an event, accomplishment, or realization that began a time of personal growth with new understanding of yourself and/or other people.

6. Write about a topic, concept or idea that makes you lose track of time because it captivates you - why do you find it so engaging?

7. When you want to learn more about something, who or what do you turn to?

*Even if you are not applying to a California college, the essay questions below are great examples of prompts you can expect **for many other schools...***

## University of California (UC)

UC applications generally offer 8 "personal insight" essay prompts to choose from. Students are required to write essays to **answer 4 of the 8 questions.**

### Essay Questions to preview – based on UC prompts:

1. Write about a leadership experience where you positively affected others, aided dispute resolution, added to longterm group efforts, etc.

2. Write about ways you express your creativity. Creativity can take multiple forms: Did you solve a problem, were you artistic in some way, did you exhibit innovative original thinking, etc.

3. Write about your greatest skill or talent, and how you developed/demonstrated this skill over a period of time.

4. How have you taken advantage of an important academic or educational opportunity? Or how did you overcome an educational challenge or barrier?

5. Write about your greatest challenge and what you did to overcome it. Share the ways this significant challenge affected your academic success.

6. Write about an academic subject you find inspiring. Share the ways you have pursued this knowledge in and/or out of school.

7. Write about how you made your community or school a better place.

8. Outside of what you have already included in your application, share why you are a strong candidate for admission to this University?

# CREATE YOUR OWN "Story Index" (continued from page 5)

MY KEY HIGHLIGHTS:                                        page:

| | |
|---|---|
| | |
| | |
| | |
| | |
| | |
| | |
| | |
| | |
| | |
| | |
| | |
| | |
| | |
| | |
| | |
| | |

CREATE YOUR OWN "Story Index"  (continued from page 5)

# CREATE YOUR OWN "Story Index"

MY KEY HIGHLIGHTS:                                    page:

| | |
|---|---|
| | |
| | |
| | |
| | |
| | |
| | |
| | |
| | |
| | |
| | |
| | |
| | |
| | |
| | |
| | |
| | |
| | |

Made in the USA
Coppell, TX
20 March 2022

75287687R00063